THE DARLINGS
Parents in Neverland

Susan Eve Haar

BROADWAY PLAY PUBLISHING INC
New York
www.broadwayplaypublishing.com
info@broadwayplaypublishing.com

Cover image by Jill Enfield
First printing: August 2006
I S B N: 978-0-88145-276-1
Book design: Marie Donovan
Word processing: Microsoft Word
Typographic controls: Ventura Publisher
Typeface: Palatino
Printed and bound in the U S A

THE DARLINGS was first performed at The Miniature Theater of Chester on 23 July 2003. The cast and creative contributors were:

MRS DARLING .... Anastasia Barzee
GEORGE .... Mark Giordano
NANA, COP, SWAMI, & JETHRO .... Andy Prosky
PORTICIA, MOTHER, & PROSPERA .... Glynis Bell

Director .... Byam Stevens
Set design .... Vicki R Davis
Lighting design .... Lara Dubin
Costume design .... Kaate Jansyn Thaw
Sound design .... Walter R Mantani
Casting .... Deborah Brown
Stage manager .... Alma Negro

CHARACTERS & SETTING

MRS DARLING, *thirty-eight. Pretty, with a palpable sexuality*

GEORGE, *forty-two. Her husband. Economic criminal, charismatic and ambitious*

DOG/NANA, GEORGE'S *shaggy confidante and a shrewd observer of human nature*

COP/MCCOOL, *thirty-four. Man on the make, publicity hound*

MOTHER, *sixties.* MRS DARLING *'s ogre of a mother*

PORTICA, *fifties. Decorator to the rich and upwardly mobile*

SWAMI, *thirty-four. Phony mystic with a fold-up turban*

JETHRO, *thirty-four. New age founder of Parents Without Children*

PROSPERA, *fifties. Former mother and co-founder of Parents Without Children.*

Time: The present

Place: New York City

Notes: All male parts may be played by the same actor with the exception of GEORGE. *All female parts may be played by the same actress with the exception of* MRS DARLING.

Scene One

(A very chic parlor and a very chic couple. Décor is Phillipe Stark. It has all the warmth of the lobby of the Royalton Hotel. Formal photo of three babies on the wall. GEORGE *is engrosssed, anxiously reading* The Wall Street Journal. MRS DARLING *completes her toilette at the hall mirror. Her back is to her husband as she speaks.)*

MRS DARLING: *(Leaning forward, looking in mirror and propping up her breasts in a bustier)* Thank God I didn't nurse! I think it's just the right tight. George? You aren't looking. You aren't even pretending to look. Well, at least I don't have one of those revolting little tummy rolls. They always show, even if you wear a girdle.

GEORGE: *(Behind the paper)* Three perfect C-section babies—Wendy, John, Michael—and only a teeny-weeny bikini scar to show for it.

MRS DARLING: Thank you, George. I'm going to pretend that you mean it. *(Looking in mirror, applying lip liner)* Every woman, at a certain age, needs liner to keep the lipstick from making those invisible lines visible. Your mother taught me that.

GEORGE: Really? She hated you.

MRS DARLING: Yes, but this was a grooming secret.

(She clicks her evening bag shut, crosses to GEORGE *and pulls the paper away.)*

GEORGE: What?

MRS DARLING: You're not ready. Not in the least ready. The car will be here in five minutes.

GEORGE: I'm not going.

MRS DARLING: That's ridiculous. Just change your shirt. Put on a blue one—there'll probably be photographers.

GEORGE: As long as they're not from the business section.

MRS DARLING: Why? Have you done something special?

GEORGE: *(Pretending to read headline)* Former Chairman and C E O George Darling indicted. Failure to disclose. Securities fraud.

MRS DARLING: Oh, George, you're such a nervous Nelly. You've done well, that's all.

GEORGE: Unusually well.

MRS DARLING: You deserve it. You're brilliant, aggressive, with the thick neck of a rutting boar.

GEORGE: A boar?

MRS DARLING: Well something full of testosterone. A bull. So, blue shirt, darling, and put on your red-striped power tie.

GEORGE: I'm not going.

MRS DARLING: Look, George, this isn't a matter of choice. It's my day, and I'm not going to walk in there without my husband.

GEORGE: Nobody's going to miss me.

MRS DARLING: That's not the point. It wouldn't look right. And besides, I want you there. I'm being honored for my hard work on behalf of the Guatemalan orphans. I've raised a lot of money, George. I've made impassioned speeches. After all, we made the war, we made the orphans. And you should see the pictures. All those children, so skinny, with those melting, brown eyes. No one else had the nerve to choose brownish children.

GEORGE: Shrewd, Honey, very shrewd.

MRS DARLING: They're presenting me with a book of the children's thank you letters, scribbled in their broken English...

GEORGE: Babe, what do you think about living in Switzerland?

MRS DARLING: Switzerland?

GEORGE: Sure, chalet in the mountains, flat in Geneva. The kids'll be bilingual, trilingual in no time. College admissions'll be a snap!

MRS DARLING: Moving?

GEORGE: Look, I can't promise you there isn't going to be a scandal. There could be some rough sledding, but in Switzerland, at least everybody's polite!

MRS DARLING: Moving?

GEORGE: Yeah, Switzerland! Skiing, and schlag. Happy little children, and that fountain gushing out of the middle of Lake Geneva! Think about it, babe, this whopper chalet with a separate children's wing.

MRS DARLING: Moving?

GEORGE: Alright, so maybe not Geneva. What's your favorite city?

MRS DARLING: Rome. I have always loved those fried zucchini blossoms, and those fountains with the dolphins and putti. Now, can we go, George?

GEORGE: I think Italy's got extradition. Let's see. *(He pulls a crumpled piece of paper out of his pocket)*

MRS DARLING: Extradition as in reciprocal legal procedures?

GEORGE: They can't get a hand on you in Switzerland.

MRS DARLING: What's going on?

GEORGE: Take a look at this one. Lucerne. Eighteen thousand square feet, nine bathrooms, primo security system

MRS DARLING: We aren't moving, George. I am about to be appointed Treasurer of the Junior League. Our children are in highly competitive and prestigious schools, and you're president of the Young President's Society. Now, are you ready?

GEORGE: It's a no-go.

MRS DARLING: I'll say please, and afterwards we can have torrid sex for hours.

GEORGE: Jesus, woman, I don't have a choice. I've got a meeting at the U S Attorney's office. But I got a ball buster lawyer from Harry. He can fix anything...

MRS DARLING: Now? It's eight o'clock on a Wednesday night. No one but the Klan has Wednesday night meetings!

GEORGE: It's either meet tonight, or walk up those steps tomorrow with a raincoat pulled over my head.

MRS DARLING: Oh, George, every time your accountant looks at you cross-eyed you think you're going to jail. (*Looking at watch*) Where's that car?

GEORGE: Maybe I'll get Allenwood. It's got golf and I've got friends there.

MRS DARLING: Stop it, George! You know you're not going to jail. And I know you're going to give in and come.

GEORGE: God, listen to me! You never listen!

(*Loud knocking at door, chauffeur*)

MRS DARLING: Just a minute, Monroe! So rude! Get up George. Now.

GEORGE: (*Checks watch*) I'm leaving in five minutes.

MRS DARLING: O.k. Just walk me in, stay a few minutes, and exit discreetly.

GEORGE: Forget it.

MRS DARLING: Is this about needing more attention? *(No response)* I admit between Michael's school applications and the brownish children I have been a bit preoccupied.

(Loud knocking at door)

MRS DARLING: JUST A MINUTE, MONROE!

(She holds out her hand. He doesn't move.)

MRS DARLING: What? What is it? Cut the crap, George!

GEORGE: Who's staying with the kids? Isn't it the nanny's day off?

MRS DARLING: Oh Christ, I completely forgot! You didn't call anyone, did you? No, of course not.

GEORGE: You got to stay.

MRS DARLING: I have an event.

GEORGE: Forget it, Babe. You're not going to just traipse out of here to some Guatemalan orphan society.

MRS DARLING: It's the Junior League. And I'm going. And you, well, you do what you want. It's not as if it's the first time they've been on their own.

(Loud knocking at door)

MRS DARLING: ALRIGHT! *(She starts to walk out)* Oh Christ! I forgot to say goodnight to the kids! *(Crossing to the intercom)* Wendy, it's Mom. Listen, honey, you're in charge. We're both going out. Read to the boys. Remember your retainer. And sweet dreams, think of cashmere cardigans. Give yourself a kiss, sweetie. See you in the morning, I love you. *(She turns on her heel. Over her shoulder)* The least you can do is wish me luck.

GEORGE: Good luck.

MRS DARLING: *(Starting to exit)* Thanks, George. You too. Chin up, and don't say anything I wouldn't say. *(She exits.)*

GEORGE: Don't worry Babe, I'm going to be fine. No problemma. *(Getting on his coat, he exits.)*

(Lights down)

Scene Two

(Lights up as GEORGE enters)

GEORGE: Hello? Honey? You here? Where the hell are you? *(Walks to door, opens it)* Nana?

(Whistles. NANA, a large shaggy dog, enters)

GEORGE: Nana. *(Kisses Nana)* You want a drink?

(GEORGE pulls out a bottle of scotch, a glass and a saucer. Pours drinks for himself and dog. Raises glass to NANA.)

GEORGE: Skol. They want to make an example of me. Flush me out of the system like some kind of sewage— Well, believe me, I'm not going down easy. Screw them all. Who do they think they're dealing with? I mean, hey, I employ eighteen hundred people. Is that sanctimonious son of a bitch thinking about them? No way. All he's thinking about is re-election. I mean, sure, I did some stuff. You got to push the envelope a little, that's how you make it happen! There's nothing I did that anybody else in my position wouldn't do! *(Takes a gulp)* The money, the money. That's all they wanna talk about. They just don't get it—money's what happens when you're making art. *(Sings to NANA)* All my hopes and schemes! All my hopes and schemes!

See, you steal because— But I didn't steal! I simply took advantage of an opportunity that was uniquely mine! And those prosecutors, those pissants, they just don't understand. Those lackies, with their badges and their forty-three thou a year, they don't know what it takes to be a master of the universe. I turned around more companies than you chewed up slippers. And when I sold, and how I sold, hey, I got friends. I play golf. I play squash. You hear things. You got instincts. You'd think they'd have something better to do. The world is not a safe place and what are they doing? They got teams of accountants, working like termites, going through my stuff. Everything. Jesus. God, you've heard it all. My one true friend. If you could talk, I'd have to put you in the shredder. Hey, just kidding. Have another. *(He kisses* NANA *affectionately.)* There would be no love in this house if it wasn't for you. So where is the love of my life? *(Looks at watch)* Out with the orphans. And she didn't even ask me what I did. Unbelievable. Hey, I could be an ax murderer as long as the Visa bill gets paid. *(Swigs)* But you know—she still gets to me. She's under my skin, like ringworm. It's amazing. After all this time, I just want to tie her up with her Gucci scarves and bang the hell out of her. But maybe wanting her's just another bad habit, you tell me. Not talking? You're one smart puppy. *(He kisses* NANA.*)* Hey, I know she's tough to live with. But, God, she can be so tender— When I first met her, she was this radiant girl, I was afraid to touch her. And she knew things. Like...how to eat an artichoke. Special. She made me feel special. Everything I wanted in one package and I thought we'd make beautiful babies together, and nothing else mattered. What happened? The girl who was my sweetheart, she's long gone. I mean she she's still here, but where's the girl I fell in love with? The girl with the elusive smile? She's shopping. *(Whispering to* NANA*)* All gone, all the love.

See, you steal because you got nothing left. *(Taking a swig, he walks over to the intercom.)*

(Banging sounds, GEORGE *shoos* NANA *out. Turns out lights and sits down.* MRS DARLING *comes blasting into the dimly lit room with balletic grace, twirling, whirling, falling into a chair. She is singing* What if God Was One of Us. *Falls from chair, gets up, flips on lights.* GEORGE *sits very still.)*

GEORGE: Still dancing?

MRS DARLING: George! My God, you scared me! Oh, you really missed something, George. What an event! It was so moving. You felt like the orphans were right there with you. And the food! These tiny Cornish hens stuffed with foie gras and cornichons...George, have you been sitting here in the dark the whole time?

*(*GEORGE *stares at her. Takes a drink)*

GEORGE: So, was it good?

MRS DARLING: Oh yes. *Magnifique.*

GEORGE: The touch of an elbow, a glance, that flirty, wispy way you have.

MRS DARLING: Oh, you are in a rotten mood.
(She stretches back in her chair, unzipping her dress.)

GEORGE: The whisper of the zipper.

MRS DARLING: Don't get maudlin, George. There wasn't an attractive man in the room. Do you want another drink? *(Getting herself one and pulling off her shoes)* George, you've been drinking with that dog again—there are paw prints on my Aubusson!

GEORGE: Those are just some...Persian leaves.

(She dances a little.)

MRS DARLING: I'll never be too old to dance. Never. Wally Nelson danced with me for hours.

GEORGE: Doesn't he shave his head and wear an earring?

MRS DARLING: He has great eyes and a great rumba.

GEORGE: Ah.

MRS DARLING: That music pulses up in me, and I have to move. I wish you'd dance with me. *(Dancing)*

GEORGE: I don't rumba.

MRS DARLING: Someday I'll be old, and alone, and fat as a walrus, but I'll still be dancing.

GEORGE: And I'll be what? Conveniently dead?

MRS DARLING: You'll be my husband, George. Whatever.

GEORGE: And what about the kids? Do they have some place in this future of yours?

MRS DARLING: The children? They'll grow up, go into analysis, and hate me. Blame me for their sexual peccadilloes and their nightmares. All parents are disappointments, eventually. *(Massaging her foot)* I really need a pedicure.

GEORGE: Is that what you need? I mean, you need oxygen, you need food, you need some kind of human connection...

MRS DARLING: I need a pedicure.

GEORGE: I need you.

MRS DARLING: I need aspirin and a lot of water.

(She walks out. We hear a door slam. GEORGE *gets up, pours another drink, he hums a waltz.)*

GEORGE: *(Yelling)* Hey, Babe? *(He yodels. Silence)* ARE YOU IN THE BATHROOM? *(Silence)* LET ME KNOW WHEN YOU'RE AVAILABLE! *(Silence)* I'm going to check on the kids.

(GEORGE exits. MRS DARLING enters in a dressing gown with a bottle of seltzer. She takes a rag and dabs at the rug. Sounds, thumping. She walks over to the intercom.)

MRS DARLING: Wendy? Honey? I know you're still awake, don't play possum with me. Oh honey, you would've been so proud of me. I brought you flowers from my table. Sweetheart roses and baby's breath. Wendy? Hello? *(Whispering)* It's O K, I know it's past your bedtime, but I love it when you wait up for me.

(GEORGE reenters.)

GEORGE: I can't find the kids.

MRS DARLING: Right.

GEORGE: They're not there.

MRS DARLING: Not funny.

GEORGE: Did you make some kind of arrangement after I left?

MRS DARLING: I left before you did.

GEORGE: Well, you could have called or something.

MRS DARLING: I was being honored. I was busy.

GEORGE: I bet they're in the kitchen!

(He exits. Banging)

MRS DARLING: *(Rifling through goody bag)* George? Don't be ridiculous, George. I locked them in myself. *(Paws through goody bag, sprays herself with perfume, wrinkles nose, takes out compact, checks self in mirror, smiles, unwraps chocolate, eats it, throws foil over shoulder)*

GEORGE: Quit the bon-bon chugging and help me look!

MRS DARLING: What's the matter with you?

GEORGE: Our children. Remember? You gave birth to them.

MRS DARLING: Yes. *(Sitting and crossing her legs)* I insisted on epidurals, but I do remember.

GEORGE: Jesus. Help me look! *(He slams out of room)*

MRS DARLING: *(Chocolate in mouth)* I LOCKED THEM IN! They're not little Houdinis.

GEORGE: Listen to me! The door was still locked, but inside, the window's open. I could see the shapes of their bodies pressed into their beds, but the room's empty. Crackling with moonlight and silence. And there's this weird stuff scattered all over. This shimmering dust. On the floor, by the windowsill. It's like some kind of phosphorescence.

MRS DARLING: Glitter. That must be it. Michael is always playing with glitter and it's impossible to get it up.

GEORGE: I rubbed a little on my fingers and it disappeared. And there was this sensation, like an electric shock.

MRS DARLING: Not glitter.

GEORGE: I looked in all the usual places. Under the bed, behind the curtains, in the tub. And then I looked in the unusual places. Up the chimney, in the garbage. Everywhere. And I can't find one of them. Christ. *(He sits down covering his eyes.)*

MRS DARLING: George?

GEORGE: What?

MRS DARLING: I just talked to Wendy.

GEORGE: You did?

MRS DARLING: I just talked to her through the intercom.

GEORGE: Did she answer?

MRS DARLING: No. But she likes to listen.

GEORGE: Christ! *(Runs out, we hear him banging)*

MRS DARLING: Really. Don't exhaust yourself, sweetheart. Look, there is a thirty-foot drop from their room. No fire escape. The house was locked, the room was locked. Where could they go?

GEORGE: I don't know! Kidnapped. Run away!

MRS DARLING: Oh, George, you are really off the deep end.

GEORGE: Wendy's friends, you know any names?

MRS DARLING: You could try her speed dial.

GEORGE: Get me the school directory.

MRS DARLING: You're going to humiliate her before her peers. That is a definite no no.

GEORGE: I have a bad feeling about this. We shouldn't have left them. Not alone. Not tonight.

MRS DARLING: They had the dog.

GEORGE: I'm calling 9-1-1.

MRS DARLING: You'd do that for them? That's so nice. But not yet. I'm going to check the linen closet. *(Exits. O S)* Come out, come out wherever you are! *(Returning)* This is not funny George. I'm scared.

GEORGE: *(Sinking into a chair)* I'm completely screwed.

MRS DARLING: We can't find our children, and everything is still about you?

GEORGE: *(Head in hands)* The stuff they're going to say. I should never have let you talk me into that twenty-three thousand dollar Renaissance toilet seat you wanted in Venice.

MRS DARLING: You could have said no.

GEORGE: How did you expect me to pay for the tennis lessons and the Canyon Ranch time-share?

MRS DARLING: Don't bullshit me, George. You're the one who needs the fancy house and all those parties to puff you up, you little man.

GEORGE: Whatever I did, I did for you and the kids.

MRS DARLING: Oh! The children! What are we going to do about our missing children?

(GEORGE *picks up phone again. Punches in three numbers*)

GEORGE: MISSING CHILDREN! (*Slaps down phone*)

MRS DARLING: Now you've done it. You didn't even give the address.

GEORGE: They trace it, babe. It's a priority.

MRS DARLING: Oh. So what do we do now?

GEORGE: Wait.

(*Pause*)

MRS DARLING: George?

GEORGE: What?

MRS DARLING: Wendy's been having these nightmares—some man with an amputated hand. No, not amputated, eaten. By an alligator. Oh George, do you think I'm the alligator?

GEORGE: (*Looking at watch*) You, sweetheart?

MRS DARLING: Maybe it's drugs. Ecstasy! Wasn't Wendy talking about dust? No, no she wouldn't do drugs. You're right. They ran away! To scare us. But why would they run away, they have everything here?

GEORGE: Uh huh.

MRS DARLING: Oh I am scared! It's so strange. So quiet. So many funny shadows. George, I looked in their room, and Michael's teddy is gone, but not one pair of shoes.

GEORGE: You really know everything they own?

MRS DARLING: YES I DO! Say it. Go ahead. Say it: I care by consumption.

GEORGE: I know. I'm the guy who pays your bills.

MRS DARLING: There must be some explanation. I know they're going to come skipping through that door, and we'll feel like total idiots.

(Doorbell)

MRS DARLING: Here they are!

(Running to door, opens door to MCCOOL*)*

MRS DARLING: Oh!... *(To* GEORGE*)* Not the kids.

MCCOOL: Detective McCool. *(Shows badge)* Nice house. Bet it looks great in print.

MRS DARLING: Why thank you! It's been in *Casa Vogue*.

MCCOOL: Super. *(Putting out hand)* George, Right? George Darling?

GEORGE: *(Shaking hands)* George Darling, my wife...

MCCOOL: Great. So people, here we are and we're gonna get to know each other real fast. I been there. You haven't. Trust me. Seven years in the field and the channel seven award for Best With The Bereaved three years in a row. Believe me, I know this is tough stuff, the toughest maybe. But we got to get that information out fast. Cause the quicker we get to an amber alert the faster we can get this story out big time and get your kids back.

GEORGE: Big time?

MCCOOL: Yeah. Priority. All of law enforcement, a media blitz, freeway signs, radio, T V news, local and national.

GEORGE: Is that absolutely necessary?

MRS DARLING: Stop thinking about yourself, George!

MCCOOL: Hey I can sympathize with you wanting a little privacy here, but at this very moment every minute counts. I don't want to scare you people but time is your worst enemy.

MRS DARLING: Why that's what my dermatologist says!

MCCOOL: *(To* GEORGE*)* Has she taken anything? No? Well she definitely should.

GEORGE: *(Getting up)* I'll get her another drink.

MCCOOL: *(Getting up and checking out intercom)* This for the servants?

MRS DARLING: Servants? Why nobody has servants anymore. You mean assistants perhaps....

GEORGE: It's for the kids.

MRS DARLING: So we don't have to raise our voices.

MCCOOL: Hey sure, it's a big house. So I take it no non-family members live here?

GEORGE: There's the dog.

MRS DARLING: People, George.

MCCOOL: And...you said kids. More than one?

GEORGE: Three. All missing.

MCCOOL: Three? Wow. Sorry. Unusual.

MRS DARLING: Unusual?

MCCOOL: Yeah.

MRS DARLING: But there was a four, that woman who drove her four children into the lake?

MCCOOL: Yeah. Look, if we get moving here we'll make today's deadline.

GEORGE: Great.

MCCOOL: So how old?

GEORGE: Wendy's twelve, Michael's seven and Johnny's our baby. Five.

MRS DARLING: No he isn't! He's still four, he's the one with the July birthday, George. A mother never forgets.

GEORGE: That's an elephant.

MRS DARLING: George!

MCCOOL: Alright. Let's work together here. I'm gonna ask you a few more questions, Mister Darling and Mrs Darling how about you go and get me some recent photos?

MRS DARLING: Photos? Well, I don't have anything recent but I had each of them photographed professionally at two.

MCCOOL: No pictures of the kids?

GEORGE: That's what she said.

MCCOOL: Anything. Snapshots.

MRS DARLING: No.

MCCOOL: Library card?

MRS DARLING: No.

MCCOOL: Hey what about school pictures? The kind you put in your wallet?

MRS DARLING: Oh I never order those! The colors are so awful and they're always out of focus, but...do you want to see their baby pictures? They were such beautiful babies. They're never quite that perfect again once they grow teeth....

MCCOOL: Drink that. *(Pointing at drink which she chugs)* Alright. Better?

MRS DARLING: Better.

MCCOOL: We can do it on a verbal....

MRS DARLING: I know! I can do a composite!

MCCOOL: That's O K...Mr. Darling. Can you give me their weights?

MRS DARLING: Wendy's eighty-seven pounds, Michaels fifty-seven pounds and Johnny's forty-seven pounds.

MCCOOL: Great. You're doing great. Hair color?

MRS DARLING: They all started blonde but it didn't last. I'd have to say...light brown.

MCCOOL: Good job.

MRS DARLING: Do you want their shoe sizes?

GEORGE: She's great with sizes.

MCCOOL: No. Height?

MRS DARLING: Oh, well Wendy can look me in the eye. If she wants to. And Michael, he's still in the under the chin club. You know, up to here? And Johnny, he's so wiggly it's hard to know how to measure...

GEORGE: Four feet.

MRS DARLING: Approximately.

MCCOOL: So Mr. Darling, exactly when did you notice your children were missing?

GEORGE: We talked to them around eight.

MCCOOL: What were they wearing?

GEORGE: Probably pajamas.

McCOOL: Probably?

MRS DARLING: It would make sense.

McCOOL: So...you didn't see them at eight?

GEORGE: No.

McCOOL: When was the last time you saw them?

GEORGE: Breakfast.

McCOOL: Breakfast?

MRS DARLING: Breakfast. Michael refused to eat frittata.

McCOOL: *(Writing on pad)* Alright. He refused to eat.
Then what?

MRS DARLING: Well...school. And after the boys have
flute and gymnastics and soccer. Wendy has Spanish
tutoring, ice-skating and ballroom dancing.

McCOOL: You drive them to school?

MRS DARLING: Why should I have a driver if he doesn't
drive?

McCOOL: Good point. After school?

GEORGE: Who knows?

MRS DARLING: Well we would have heard from
somebody if there were a problem.

McCOOL: O K. At dinner?Anything unusual happen at
dinner?

GEORGE: We were out.

MRS DARLING: We both had appointments.

McCOOL: So—you, him—neither of you was home?

MRS DARLING: Look, Detective you don't seem to
understand our situation. I had a very important
function to attend. You'll see it in the Sunday Style
Section! And George...

MCCOOL: *(Putting up his hand)* Hey! You got every right to go out. We're not living in the stone age. You got to have your own life. Yeah, in fact I sympathize, I mean torn between your social responsibilities and your kids...

MRS DARLING: That's it exactly! You see George?

MCCOOL: You talk to the sitter?

MRS DARLING: The sitter? There was no sitter.

MCCOOL: Wait a minute...they were completely alone?

GEORGE: Look, we're not on trial here.

MCCOOL: No! No! Look, buddy, I want to get this story out as much as you do. I just gotta get the story...

GEORGE: We were only gone...

MRS DARLING: Maybe an hour. Right George? You were home before me...

GEORGE: Less than an hour.

MCCOOL: Great. Now we're cookin with gas. *(Looking at watch and speeding up speech)* When you got home George, did you happen to look at your watch when you checked on the kids?

GEORGE: Not exactly. I had the lights out for a bit. I was...napping.

MRS DARLING: George!

GEORGE: I wasn't feeling well. So I turned out the lights and I was lying on the sofa.

MRS DARLING: You're lying George!

MCCOOL: What makes you think that?

MRS DARLING: I saw the footprints! He was drinking with the dog again!

MCCOOL: The dog?

GEORGE: She has the blood of champions.

McCOOL: Alright. Hey, it's O K, a guy deserves a drink at the end of a hard day. So you were drinking?

GEORGE: Lightly.

MRS DARLING: THERE IS NO MORE SCOTCH!

GEORGE: That dog is a camel!

McCOOL: And you had the lights off.

GEORGE: Only part of the time.

MRS DARLING: It's your fault George! You were drinking your troubles away and you let them come into our house and steal my babies!

GEORGE: Look, you're the one who had to go get honored.

McCOOL: Cut it out people. You both went out. You left a dog in charge. George gets home and he's drinking...

GEORGE: Lightly.

McCOOL: With the dog. And then what, you get home?

MRS DARLING: I had a drink.

McCOOL: And then after you checked the kids...

MRS DARLING: Actually it was George.

McCOOL: How much later?

MRS DARLING: I don't know.

McCOOL: Fifteen minutes? An hour?

GEORGE: More like fifteen minutes.

MRS DARLING: That's right! Not long at all! And we had no reason to worry. They've taken care of themselves on many occasions before and they've never disappeared!

McCOOL: Uh huh.

MRS DARLING: And the reason we took a little while to call you...well I thought I was talking to Wendy right after I got home, I thought that she was listening...

MCCOOL: Through the intercom.

MRS DARLING: Yes.

MCCOOL: And then you went to look...

GEORGE: Sure!

MCCOOL: Looked in the bedrooms?

GEORGE: Of course!

MCCOOL: Searched the whole house?

GEORGE: We're not idiots.

MCCOOL: Bathroom hampers?

MRS DARLING: I looked myself!

MCCOOL: Sure you looked everywhere?

GEORGE: Yes we looked everywhere—under the beds, in the closets, hell, we even looked in the furnace!

MCCOOL: The furnace?

MRS DARLING: Of course we didn't expect to find them there! Don't you see? We're the victims and you make us sound so...irresponsible!

MCCOOL: Let me try this again. One family picture. Maybe a Christmas card? No? Kwanzaa?

MRS DARLING: Don't they give you people some kind of sensitivity training?

GEORGE: You know, McCool, I pay enough taxes in one year for you to retire forever.

MCCOOL: Look, buddy, I'm gonna overlook that. In fact, I'm not even gonna try to guess what you mean. Because that would really piss me off and I didn't get up this morning at six and shine my shoes and put on this tie to come here and get pissed off or to waste my time talking about some rotten rich kids who took off for Bermuda without leaving a note!

MRS DARLING: It's not their fault they're gone!

GEORGE: You got a problem with us fine. But this is for the kids.

McCOOL: So give me something.

MRS DARLING: Mikey has a scar on his upper right arm. From that vicious lab.

GEORGE: It was a Chow. The ones with the blue tongues.

MRS DARLING: And...Johnny oh he has the sweetest laugh...

McCOOL: That's it?

MRS DARLING: Isn't that enough?

GEORGE: Just...get started!

McCOOL: *(Standing)* Yeah? And do what?

GEORGE: Whatever the hell is going to get the kids back! I don't care if you plaster my picture from coast to coast!

McCOOL: The kids? I don't think so. No bikes in the doorway. No backpacks by the door...

MRS DARLING: Backpacks! They're terrible for the spine!

McCOOL: Eleven thousand four hundred and sixty abductions a year and I get you.

GEORGE: He doesn't believe us.

McCOOL: I don't believe you.

MRS DARLING: How dare you! You want to see my Caesarean scar?

McCOOL: Isn't that a tummy tuck?

MRS DARLING: I DO FIVE HUNDRED SIT-UPS A WEEK! I earned this belly!

GEORGE: Get the hell out of this house!

MRS DARLING: George! No! We need his help! Look detective, please try to understand. We do have children. They are missing. And if we are not altogether in command of the facts...well so I'm not a perfect mother. I admit it. Yes I have my own life. Yes I go out on occasion. Yes I keep my distance...

GEORGE: Hey, babe, you don't have to apologize for anything.

MRS DARLING: Thank you, George, but I need him to understand. I did my best. I never hurt one of them. Not a fall from a high chair or...or a finger crushed in the door. Not a scar on any of them, doesn't that count for something? You see...I love my children. I love them with ferocity. I would die for them. Just not slowly.

MCCOOL: Bravo. *(He claps and starts to go.)*

GEORGE: Hey! *(He gets up to keep him there.)*

MCCOOL: Better not. I'm in a bad mood and I got backup outside.

(GEORGE hesitates, steps back and MCCOOL exits.)

MRS DARLING: Oh my God. What do we do now?

GEORGE: I don't know.

MRS DARLING: But you always know. That's why I married you.

GEORGE: Alright. I can do this. I'll find them. I'll do it myself. They're my kids too. At least I think they are, and I'm going to find them. And I'm taking Nana. I know you hate her, but she's part bloodhound and she loves them like a mother.

MRS DARLING: George...

GEORGE: Until I'm back, don't open that door for anyone who doesn't have a badge.

MRS DARLING: George?

(GEORGE *exits.*)

GEORGE: *(Calling)* NANA!

(Lights down. End of Scene Two)

Scene Three

(Lights up on MRS DARLING *collapsed on a chair, weeping. She takes a shot glass, tosses back three successive slugs. The doorbell rings. She jumps up, checks herself out in the mirror. She goes to the door, puts on the chain lock and opens it cautiously.)*

MRS DARLING: I want to see a badge, a warrant and a picture I D.

PORTICA: A picture I D? They're always so hideous.

MRS DARLING: *(Flinging open the door)* Portica, Thank God!

PORTICA: Another decorating emergency? The wallpaper moving in on you? I had a client like that once. It was either tear that paper down, or into the looney bin!

MRS DARLING: Portica, my children are gone.

PORTICA: Gone?

MRS DARLING: Vanished.

PORTICA: Let's have a drink. I see this is a night for anesthetic.

MRS DARLING: You have no idea.

PORTICA: What can I do?

MRS DARLING: You can do anything. You work miracles. Everybody says so.

PORTICA: Well, we can get the children's wing going.

MRS DARLING: I need something now!

PORTICA: We could double up on crews...

MRS DARLING: NO!

PORTICA: Look I feel for you, I really do. But, it's the middle of the night and shouldn't you be calling the police?

MRS DARLING: We did. But they didn't believe us!

PORTICA: So unhelpful, though you pay those oodles of taxes! But don't worry, darling, you'll find them. They haven't flown off like little birds.

MRS DARLING: Tell me what to do!

PORTICA: How should I know? I was hoping to discuss the height of the room dividers.

MRS DARLING: I'm just mortified....

PORTICA: Honey, it's nothing to be embarrassed about. Why everyone loses a child from time to time...

MRS DARLING: Not me.

PORTICA: Of course not!

MRS DARLING: But now, what will everyone think? I am just riddled with guilt and anxiety!

PORTICA: (Looking in her bag) Here. Oh Christ! I'm out of valium!

MRS DARLING: I took all of George's Xanax.

PORTICA: Look, everybody's losing their children. It's nothing to be ashamed of. If it's not a custody dispute, it's drugs, bulimia, or gender confusion. But they always turn up—eventually.

MRS DARLING: When?

PORTICA: When? Who knows?

MRS DARLING: You don't think that's a problem?

PORTICA: Well it's all a matter of perspective.

MRS DARLING: It is not! People agree on this. Everyone
thinks that children are important. Because children are
the cornerstone of family, and family is the cornerstone
of civilization!

PORTICA: Alright. I admit it. It is upsetting. And you
never know what people are going to think. But
children are messy, demanding, over-rated and damn
expensive. You can do without them.

MRS DARLING: NO! I can't. They're my statement,
my defining moment. I can't go on without them!

PORTICA: I know, you were very fond of them. Still,
such lovely memories, why pollute them with reality?

MRS DARLING: Because it's just not O K. Losing an
earring is O K, but not your children!

PORTICA: Alright, just try to calm down.

MRS DARLING: How can I? I made them and
now...they're gone! I'm being sucked into an abyss of
my own invention!

PORTICA: Well, I'm sure it's very difficult, so just push
it back. Or let it roll over you, and come out the other
side. Breathe. Oxygen, that's the thing. That's it. How's
that? Are we feeling better?

MRS DARLING: Better.

PORTICA: Good. Now close your eyes.

MRS DARLING: Darkness. I feel like I'm tumbling
through a reality I once knew. Everywhere is darkness,
disaster.

PORTICA: You poor thing! A quick color consult? Never be afraid of color.

MRS DARLING: It's russets this year, right? Umbers and oranges...why I was thinking...thanks, but not now.

PORTICA: (*Massaging* MRS DARLING's *shoulders*) Look, this is not the first time you've peered over the edge, right? Remember when the caterer ran out of fish?

MRS DARLING: Humiliating.

PORTICA: But you survived. You're resilient. It's going to be fine. Just close your eyes and breath. Come on. Breathe. That's it. That's it. Relax.

MRS DARLING: How can I? I'm lost! Unless...there's a miracle!

PORTICA: Honey I create them every day. Let me get you a pillow.

MRS DARLING: Thank you. What next?

PORTICA: Keep breathing. In—one two three, out— one two three. That's it, relax. Are we relaxed?

MRS DARLING: Better.

PORTICA: Good. Because I brought a treat. Get ready. I'm spreading out the plans, and you will look and you will be delighted, and all doubt will leave your heart. You'll be admired and envied.

MRS DARLING: (*Looking at plans*) Oh the pool! Sapphire tiles how perfect!

PORTICA: The material world is only the reflection of the inner state, but given time, the exterior seeps in and rearranges the psychic furniture.

MRS DARLING: It does?

PORTICA: Come on, let's build it.

MRS DARLING: I can't.

PORTICA: Admired and envied. Admired and envied. Illuminated in envy. Like moonlight.

MRS DARLING: Don't you understand? My kids are gone! Why do I need a kid's wing now?

PORTICA: You don't need kids for a kid's wing! It has to be built. It has its own inevitability. And then...the children will have to come back! Because they are the natural inhabitants of the children's wing!

MRS DARLING: What if they don't? How are we going to live without them?

PORTICA: I have no idea. But look, I brought samples. Aquamarine jacquard, and pink silk for the couch. Visualize the couch, curved like a conch shell, and just that tinge of coral.

MRS DARLING: *(Examining plans)* Oh! It's like a magical island. Like a cave. Mermaids. And so safe, so very safe. Oh, we'll never be able to build this!

PORTICA: Don't you like it?

MRS DARLING: I love it, I love it.

PORTICA: Too gaudy? Too West Indies?

MRS DARLING: *(Shaking head)* No, no.

PORTICA: Cost? We could always cut the waterfall.

MRS DARLING: No children. Oh Portica, have you ever had something you didn't know you loved just vanish?

PORTICA: Well, I once lost a signed Lalique ashtray during a party.

MRS DARLING: I am talking about my children!

PORTICA: Alright, I understand it's upsetting. But I'm sure they'll be back. And then they'll have their own space. An additional eight thousand square feet, plenty of room for independence or interaction. In fact, they'll want to come back as soon as they see the plans! By the way, I did bring a short contract and authorization form.

(MRS DARLING *bursts into tears.*)

PORTICA: Did I say something wrong?

MRS DARLING: I never knew I could feel this much.

PORTICA: So, in some ways it's a growth experience.

MRS DARLING: Really?

PORTICA: You'll survive. And with time, this terror will only be a shadow in your peripheral vision. All will be well, and we will build an irresistible children's wing.

MRS DARLING: How am I supposed to continue?

PORTICA: Have you eaten? Try white food.

MRS DARLING: Rice?

PORTICA: Coconut ice cream, undercooked French toast, tofu. And honey get some sleep. You look terrible.

MRS DARLING: I can't! I'm waiting!

PORTICA: Just a few minutes. Here.

(PORTICA *pulls together two armchairs, leads her to them, lies her down gently, removes her shoes, and covers her with an afghan.*)

MRS DARLING: You're going to leave me!

PORTICA: *(Whispering)* I'm not leaving, I'm going. Relax! That's it! Sleep.
    The children's wing. Visualize! It's inside your mind's eye. A place where you are always loved. A magic place, no budget, no contractor. Yes, sleep, my darling, then sign on the line. A one third deposit builds your babies a nest. Venetian glass tile, glimmering like scales, stuttering aquamarine walls and a pool big enough to have its own tides. Build it and they will come back,

sucked out of a fairytale by the magnetism of the material. Build it, and they will forgive you.

MRS DARLING: *(Sleeping)* Build it. Forgive me.

(She turns down the light and gently exits.)

(End of Scene Three)

Scene Four

(MRS DARLING lies dreaming. Sits bolt upright into her dream)

MRS DARLING: MAMA! MAMA!

MOTHER: I'm right here, baby. Shhhh.

MRS DARLING: Oh, Mama, is that really you?

MOTHER: Mama is here. I'm right here.

MRS DARLING: Mama. I need you. Help me.

MOTHER: I know, honey. Mama's going to fix everything. There's my girl. My baby girl. Mama will make it all O K. *(Singing)*
Hush little baby, don't say a word,
Mama's going to buy you a mocking bird,
And if that mocking bird don't sing,
Mama's going to chop off its shiny wing
And if that mocking bird don't fly,
Mama's gonna leave you high and dry

MRS DARLING: Mama? *(Reaching for her)*

MOTHER: Don't touch! Never never, you bad girl, you little leech. Look at the marks! Leechmarks from your suck suck teeth. But I pull you off, I burn you with my little match, and you let go, good girl, and all that's left is a little mark.

MRS DARLING: Who are you?

MOTHER: Why your mother!

MRS DARLING: Then help me!

MOTHER: You think Mama took the kids to save them from you?

MRS DARLING: You always took everything I loved!

MOTHER: I don't have them, I can't stand children.

MRS DARLING: But you do know something. You do.

MOTHER: Three sweet children. Far, far, far away.

MRS DARLING: Oh please, if you ever felt anything for me, help me find my babies.

MOTHER: Never never never land!

MRS DARLING: Please.

MOTHER: Nothing for nothing, sweetie.

MRS DARLING: Anything. What do you want? Jewelry? Here, take my ring. Six-carat gemicological institute guarantee. Please, just give me a clue.

MOTHER: It looks like paste.

MRS DARLING: Oh, cut it out, mother. Tell me something real or give me back the ring!

MOTHER: John's teddy...

MRS DARLING: Yes?

MOTHER: He ate all the fur off. The eyes are gone and its got a magic-markered nose.

MRS DARLING: You do know!

MOTHER: Maybe, baby.

MRS DARLING: Are they safe? Please let them be O K. Oh God, I hope they're not scared. They do get scared, though they pretend to be so brave. Is Wendy taking care of the boys?

MOTHER: Yes.

MRS DARLING: Oh thank God! Thank you, mother. Thank you.

MOTHER: I'll take those earrings.

(MRS DARLING *hands one earring to* MOTHER.)

MRS DARLING: Are they someplace in the City?

MOTHER: No.

MRS DARLING: How could they get out of town in so little time? Did they fly?

MOTHER: You always were very clever.

MRS DARLING: *(Handing her the other earring)* Oh, mother, here! It's all I have left. Please, I need to find them. I need them to forgive me, I need to love them. Help me find them.

MOTHER: No.

MRS DARLING: Then why are you here?

MOTHER: I'm here to harvest your organs.

MRS DARLING: *(Backing away)* What?

MOTHER: Extra parts. Mine are wearing out.

MRS DARLING: What?

MOTHER: Come on honey. I need your—liver, liver, liver. Oh, damn, I can smell it—I forgot about the drinking. Alright, alright, just one little kidney. Won't kill you anyway. You'll barely notice. And I'll take your eyes, your lovely eyes. Come here honey! Don't hide from mother! Oh you bad, bad, selfish girl. Why, I can barely see out of these old eyes. Come to Momma! Let me to see you through your own eyes.

MRS DARLING: You sucked the love out of me, and now you want me for spare parts?

(She leaps on her mother attempting to strangle her. They struggle.)

MOTHER: Oh! Look what I found! Your heart! So cleverly made, four chambers—one for each baby and one just for me.

MRS DARLING: Give it back!

MOTHER: *(Tossing it in the air)* You don't really need it, and I can use a spare.

MRS DARLING: I NEED MY HEART! I'm going to find my children and love them!

MOTHER: Oh right. When toads wear rubber boots. You'll find them? Oh come on, give Mama just one little organ, and she'll help.

MRS DARLING: Alright, you can have a kidney. Just give me a clue.

MOTHER: A small clue for a small kidney?

MRS DARLING: Yes.

MOTHER: Just look in the mirror, honey. It's always been your only map.

MRS DARLING: What? Where are they?

MOTHER: *(Laughing)* Never never neverland.

MRS DARLING: No!

MOTHER: *(Fading)* I told you sweetie! Never say never !

MRS DARLING: Please! I'll build you an altar. I'll sacrifice goats!

MOTHER: That would be nice. But no. *(Fading)*

Don't worry about the kids. I'll take good care of them!

(MRS DARLING wakes screaming.)

Scene Five

(GEORGE *reenters without* NANA.)

GEORGE: Nothing. Not a clue, unless you count this shred of teddy bear that Nana found. I even tried the cops again. Can you believe it, babe? I went to the station and they took me to the morgue. *(Pours a drink and slugs it back)* Big bodies, little bodies, I tell you, you can't get out of this life alive.

MRS DARLING: George, it's my mother. She took the kids.

GEORGE: Oh honey, give it up. She was an old vulture, but she's been dead sixteen years.

MRS DARLING: She said she did. And I recognized her, the cruelty, the bad breath, the sheer undertow of the woman.

GEORGE: Honey, it was a dream. Message from the sponsor. Forget it. Now, we have to make some big decisions, very quickly, with imperfect facts. One, can we find the kids? Two, do they want to be found? Three, are they in a more fucked up place than this? And four, what about me? I'm running out of time here.

MRS DARLING: SHE WANTED TO HARVEST MY ORGANS! Oh my God, I think she took the kids for spare parts. You know. Genetically compatible spare parts?

GEORGE: Look, she's dead. Stop it! Come here. *(Embracing her)* What a night.

MRS DARLING: What a night.

GEORGE: Oh bunny, I'm so sorry. So sorry I have to go.

MRS DARLING: It's been years since you called me bunny.

GEORGE: Sweetheart, still my sweetheart.

MRS DARLING: Oh!

(He begins to undress her.)

MRS DARLING: Honey? What about the kids?

(GEORGE is kissing her neck)

MRS DARLING: No, yes, but not now.

GEORGE: Oh don't worry about the kids.

(She holds onto him limply while he tries to get her interested.)

GEORGE: Aren't you in the mood, honey? Headache?

(He attempts to wrap her legs around his waist while she commences wilting toward the floor.)

MRS DARLING: Not now. I'm waiting.

GEORGE: Look, I've been waiting, holding my breath every goddam minute since I realized they were gone. I mean, I have a right to want to breathe, and eat, and make love to my wife, even if they never come back!

(He attempts to embrace her.)

MRS DARLING: *(Falling to the floor)* I'm exhausted. I'm aging by the minute, I can feel it, I can positively feel it, the pull of gravity against my skin. NOT NOW!

GEORGE: Let me in, Babe.

MRS DARLING: Now? In the face of disaster you develop a sudden interest in the lack of intimacy in our marriage? OUR CHILDREN, GEORGE. For god's sake, George, you planted them, they grew inside me! Nine times three! I didn't touch alcohol for twenty-nine months. And who would I be without them?

GEORGE: Yourself, babe.

MRS DARLING: We have to find them.

GEORGE: Look, I made calls to important men with sleazy connections. I offered money, I gave bribes. I had conversations with prostitutes, and transvestites, and transvestite prostitutes. I did the right thing!

MRS DARLING: You did, sweetie.

GEORGE: Have you thought anymore about Switzerland?

MRS DARLING: No.

GEORGE: Well I have.

MRS DARLING: What does that mean?

GEORGE: When you get the kids, you join me.

MRS DARLING: You want me to stay? And you're going to leave. With whatever we've got?

GEORGE: It's not like I don't still want you with me. You're my life's companion, my only historian. No one else remembers what I looked like naked at twenty.

MRS DARLING: Is that love?

GEORGE: Come with me now, before it's too late.

MRS DARLING: I can't just give up.

GEORGE: Look, I want you with me, but I got to go.

MRS DARLING: I keep thinking they're going to walk back in.

GEORGE: Maybe they will, but I can't wait.

MRS DARLING: I know we haven't done everything. There must be something else.

GEORGE: What do you want to do?

MRS DARLING: Maybe they're just out of sight. In some kind of blind spot. My mother said never-never land.

GEORGE: Forget about your mother. Come on, babe, we don't have time to waste, there are just so many hours in a day when you can do international wire transfers.

MRS DARLING: Just let me try to find the kids first. Please. We have to finish this thing and then I'll go with you.

GEORGE: I'm taking a big chance. They're on my tail.

MRS DARLING: One last try and then I'm yours.

GEORGE: But will you be with me? Really be with me? Take showers with me, and hold my arm on the street?

MRS DARLING: Yes.

GEORGE: Promise?

MRS DARLING: Cross my heart, hope to die, stick a needle in my eye.

GEORGE: Swear to it?

MRS DARLING: On my children.

GEORGE: Alright.

MRS DARLING: Oh thank you thank you! George, what's that number? They are endlessly advertising and they have that little jingle. 1 800 Dial-A-Spirit? *(She dials.)* Emanations? Yes. Missing persons? Certainly. Voice vibrations? Yes. Runes? What are runes? Never mind. We'll take it all. What? Wonderful. *(To GEORGE)* They said they'll be here right away.

(SWAMI throws the door open.)

SWAMI: Right address? *(Checking his beeper)*

| GEORGE | MRS DARLING: |
| I guess. | YES! |

SWAMI: I am Swami Vishnu Averishnu.

MRS DARLING: Thank you for coming!

SWAMI: No master card, no visa, cash is good.
And who is the responsible billing party?

GEORGE: Me.

SWAMI: But I detect flight. Right?

MRS DARLING: Cash. Come on, George.

(GEORGE *starts counting out bills.*)

SWAMI: Thank-you.

GEORGE: Do I get a receipt?

MRS DARLING: Oh George. Help us find our children.

SWAMI: Children who want to disappear have a way
of staying lost.

MRS DARLING: Why would they want to stay lost?

SWAMI: The house has not been violated. I sense no
struggle. Your children are gone of their own free will.

MRS DARLING: Oh!

GEORGE: I told you. Forget it, babe.

SWAMI: *(Throwing cards in the air catches one)* The knight
of wands! He charges on, cudgel in hand. The cudgel
sprouts leaves, knobby as a phallus. Look at this card!
The horse's eyes roll back, and the rider can hardly stay
on!

(Showing it to MRS DARLING*)*

MRS DARLING: Oh! That's you George, the resemblance
is uncanny! But this is not about George, Swami. I think
my mother knows where my children are, but she
won't tell. The She-god of the dead. She would suck the
blood out of their umbilical chords just to plump up her
face.

SWAMI: You want me to summon her?

MRS DARLING: I think she has them, she always took everything I loved.

GEORGE: She's dead.

SWAMI: I have had battles with she demons and the walking dead. I can reach into the river of death and pluck her out, if I need to.

GEORGE: Is this going to take long?

SWAMI: As long as it takes the minnow to escape the net. Ah, what has slipped through? Not a fish. It's... a crow! *(He crows.)* Lost boys away into the neverland.

MRS DARLING: He knows!

SWAMI: Sure, I can see the emanations. In full living color. When was the last time you ate?

MRS DARLING: I don't know.

SWAMI: A little bird? Tiny boned and delicate. I feel its fear.

MRS DARLING: The Cornish hen! You see George?

GEORGE: Spooky.

SWAMI: *(Holding up cards)* Look! The cards are a mirror, an empty pool, into which we toss the essence of our being. We see only our reflection, rippling round the spirit. Knock on the door of the spirits. Knock knock!

GEORGE: Can you predict the hour of my arrest?

MRS DARLING: Don't be selfish, George!

SWAMI: I feel the presence of a child....

MRS DARLING: Oh! You do? Really?

SWAMI: A woman, or a child.

MRS DARLING: Just one? We're missing three.

GEORGE: Swami Averishnu, how long is this going
to take?

SWAMI: I'm going, as fast as I can, but there are
distances to cross, the drifting plains of the dead,
the pink expanse of time.

GEORGE: Double if you finish it up in the next ten
minutes.

SWAMI: Cash?

GEORGE: Cash.

SWAMI: *(He begins to talk very fast holding out cards.)*
Choose a card any card, that's it, baby! Monkey!
Look what she chose! Ten of wands that's excessive
pressure. Obstacles, delays, disasters.
    Oh, now I feel her! I feel her! Like a storm, a
maelstrom. Yes! A frigid neglect that cauterizes
all feeling!

MRS DARLING: That's my mother! No, Swami no!
Please, not her! I want my daughter back. Not my
mother!

SWAMI: I feel...an organ in need of replacement.
Does your mother have a compromised liver?

MRS DARLING: That's her! Get rid of her!

SWAMI: Flee! Back to the lower intestine of the devil
you cancerous polyp! You evil mollusk, you venomous
spirit reeking of toxic mold.
    BE GONE, be gone! Release this woman and return
her children, reel them in like kites from the night sky!
Wendy is that you? Speaks to us! Speak!

GEORGE: Jesus what a bullshit artist! I cannot believe I
am paying for this. Cut the crap, Swami! Do you know
where the kids are?

SWAMI: Wendy uses talcum powder with a yellow
flower scent.

GEORGE: Yes or no, it's a simple question. Here, maybe this will help you. The dog found it. *(Holds out scrap of teddy bear)*

SWAMI: *(Taking it, sniffing)* Delirium, frenzy. Perplexity. Thirteen. Destiny. Fate, advancement for better or worse. Sad girl. Broken sequence. Interruption. What is with thirteen? Oh, there's a smell of nasturtium! It's Wendy! Welcome!

GEORGE: Jesus! I'm hearing something! *(Mimicking SWAMI)* Wendy? Wendy! It's Wendy !

MRS DARLING: WENDY! Where?

GEORGE: Wendy? Where are you, honey?

MRS DARLING: George, can you really hear her? THERE IS NO ONE HERE!

GEORGE: I can hear her. You she's given up on.

MRS DARLING: But why can't I hear her? Swami?

SWAMI: What?

MRS DARLING: Is there some kind of volume control?

SWAMI: Voice vibrations from another world, faint as possum tracks.

GEORGE: Yeah. Muffled. Like cheesecloth.

MRS DARLING: Cheesecloth? Oh George, I don't believe you.

GEORGE: Suit yourself, babe.

MRS DARLING: Do you really hear her? Or are you torturing me? *(To Wendy)* HE NEVER EVEN WANTED YOU! But I do. Please, talk to me. Honey? I can't hear you but here's a quick kiss for you and the boys.*(Blows kisses)* Hi Johnny, my sweetie boy, and Michael, you handsome little guy.

SWAMI: Wendy, we need to know where you are.

GEORGE: *(To* MRS DARLING*)* Wendy? She says...
they're in some place that's off the map.

MRS DARLING: Very exclusive. How are we going to
find it?

GEORGE: They'll find us. After all, they left, they can
come back when they goddam please. Right Swami?

SWAMI: Perhaps. Perhaps not.

GEORGE: Anyway, Wendy's here. So you can stop
worrying.

MRS DARLING: Here? In spirit? Oh George, does that
mean that she's dead?

GEORGE: No, for Christ's sake. It just means...
(To SWAMI*)* What does it mean?

SWAMI: Her spirit is troubled. She has fled to a place
where not a thorn will stain her beauty. You have
forgotten the rituals.

GEORGE: What could be that important?

MRS DARLING: Why don't you ask her, George.
You're the one with the open channel!

SWAMI: Divinatory meaning, unfavorable news.

GEORGE: Don't worry we'll fix it, whatever it is.

SWAMI: *(Holding up card)* See? Three swords piercing
a heart.

MRS DARLING: I feel it! We forgot something crucial!

GEORGE: Alright, so we forgot something. The ritual.

SWAMI: Yes.

GEORGE: Baby, what the hell did we forget?

MRS DARLING: How should I know?

GEORGE: Her flute concert?

SWAMI: No that's in May.

GEORGE: Give us a hint.

SWAMI: Pink icing with little blue roses.

GEORGE: What?

MRS DARLING: Wendy has always loved sweetheart roses.

SWAMI: Icing.

MRS DARLING: Her birthday! We forgot her birthday!

SWAMI: Thirteen!

MRS DARLING: Swami, tell her to come back and we will have the biggest party! Or the smallest. Just us, just the family if that's what she wants. (Calling) WHATEVER YOU WANT WENDY! (She runs to the intercom) Wendy? Wendy? Please talk to me. You have every right to be angry. You have feelings, we all do. I know I have not been a picture perfect mommy. I know I have been selfish and I have pushed you away. But I love you. And I can change. Oh honey, I'm different already. Cross my heart, hope to die, stick a needle through my eye. (She hums the Hush Little Baby tune.) Everything will be different. We will take vacations together. We will have family dinners. Wendy! Talk to me! I'm your mother!

GEORGE: Swami. Tell her.

SWAMI: Such is the nature of the battleground that the bells are never silent.

GEORGE: Right. You see, you'll always hear her. In your heart of hearts. Never silent. And if there is a battleground, hey, who says it has to be in this world? I mean, I'm not saying the kids are gone from this world, oh no. It's just...

SWAMI: She can fly.

GEORGE: Right. She can fly, and now she wants to learn to ski. Switzerland is looking good!

MRS DARLING: Is she going to come back?

GEORGE: No.

MRS DARLING: No!

SWAMI: George? My beeper is going to go off. George, the F B I. They're not waiting. You've got...extremely limited time. I see a cell and a nice man—no not a nice man—named Leroi who wants you to be his wife. I see snow capped mountains!

GEORGE: The Alps.

(Beeper goes off.)

SWAMI: Ah hah.

GEORGE: HOW LONG?

SWAMI: Without the cash, all is ephemera.

GEORGE: Alright! *(Pulling out cash)*

SWAMI: Half an hour give or take. Hasta la vista.

MRS DARLING: But the children!

SWAMI: Never too late, you make your fate. *(He is out the door.)*

MRS DARLING: Wait! Oh. Oh my God, what are we going to do?

GEORGE: Look, I got to go too, babe. It's not going to be Leroi.

MRS DARLING: Go? But the children.

GEORGE: We could try again.

MRS DARLING: Try again?

GEORGE: Look, you love them, I love them. But we screwed the kids up. You know it as well as I do. It's

like pancakes, you always ruin the first batch.
Throw them out! Start again.

MRS DARLING: This is family. You can't give up.

GEORGE: There's no kind of family here. You know it.
And the kids know it.

MRS DARLING: You're wrong. This is their home! Oh,
and George, we have to build a new wing on the beach
house. With water and mermaids. They'll have to come
back.

GEORGE: Honey, we lost them on the turn, way back.

MRS DARLING: Don't you understand? Without them,
I'm nothing.

GEORGE: Sure it's sad. I mean, we'll always love
them, we'll always think of them, but this is a real
opportunity to try again and do it right!

MRS DARLING: I'm thirty-eight, George. I don't want
to start again.

GEORGE: I can understand that. So if you don't want to
do the pregnancy thing, we can rent a womb! Or adopt!
Who says we've got such good genes? Take a look at
John's overbite sometime. Seriously, have you ever
considered they're better off without us? Think about it.
This is the best thing for everybody.

MRS DARLING: Michael is five. It's hard to believe he
needs a clean start.

GEORGE: What about Wendy?

MRS DARLING: I forgot to love her.

GEORGE: And now you would?

MRS DARLING: Yes. Even if I have to face her and admit
that I am getting old. And I am, George. But I will revel
in the beauty of my daughter.

GEORGE: Is that love?

MRS DARLING: If it isn't it's as close as I can get.

GEORGE: Look, I'm out of here. The F B I's on my tail, and I'm not doing my waiting in a cell.

MRS DARLING: And how am I going to talk to Wendy without you?

GEORGE: I don't know. You'll have to find your own way.

MRS DARLING: What do you recommend? A séance?

GEORGE: Just open your heart and wait. Look, I got to go.

MRS DARLING: Wait? Oh, honey.

(She starts to rub his shoulders.)

GEORGE: Feels good. But I got to pack.

MRS DARLING: Your shoulders...

GEORGE: Your fingers. Nice.

MRS DARLING: Yes.

GEORGE: I've only got a few minutes.

MRS DARLING: Remember that pink bed in Mexico?

GEORGE: Thought I'd died and gone to heaven.

MRS DARLING: You don't have to go right away.

GEORGE: Soon.

MRS DARLING: Relax.

(She starts unbuttoning his shirt.)

GEORGE: Now?

MRS DARLING: Let's make another batch.

GEORGE: Gotta be quick.

MRS DARLING: George?

GEORGE: Mmmmh?

MRS DARLING: You wouldn't lie to me.

GEORGE: About what?

MRS DARLING: You do hear Wendy.

GEORGE: Mmmh?

MRS DARLING: You're really going to go?

GEORGE: You want me to go to jail?

MRS DARLING: No.

GEORGE: Look, honey, if I could do anything, believe me I would. But I just got to move on. The kids are O K and Wendy has a hell of a lot of experience taking care of stuff on her own. They'll be O K.

MRS DARLING: What about me?

GEORGE: Your passport's upstairs.

MRS DARLING: But I can't give up. I know I can be a real mother. I know I can make it right. The boys, well, boys are easy to please—Little League tryouts, a few sleepovers and s'mores.

GEORGE: What about Wendy?

MRS DARLING: I know you think you know what it's like for me. But you don't. When I look in the mirror, all I see is my mother looking back. It's horrible, George. I'm gone, absolutely erased. I have erased my face and there's nothing left but the grin. Nothing left of me. I've been fighting it. I have been so desperate, so alone.

GEORGE: Come on, babe, you go out six nights a week.

MRS DARLING: I need to! To preserve my sanity. I need the boards, the exercise classes, the book club.

GEORGE: So you've become your mother.

MRS DARLING: Yes. And I have driven my children away, and without them I have no chance. No chance.

GEORGE: They'll come back when they're good and ready.

MRS DARLING: Do you think so? Oh George, did Wendy say that? Did she? Is this just some kind of nightmare, some trial by ordeal? Can I win her back?

GEORGE: You will or you won't. That much is for sure.

MRS DARLING: But now what?

GEORGE: Ready?

MRS DARLING: You're going?

GEORGE: Yes.

MRS DARLING: You can't just walk away!

GEORGE: Watch me, babe. You think you need me now, but you don't need me. You never really did. You think that this is it, but when it comes right down to it, nothing is unbearable.

MRS DARLING: It's unbearable to lose a child. To lose three...well, I'll never make it alone.

GEORGE: You could survive anything.

MRS DARLING: Not this.

GEORGE: Look, they'll come back. Just hang in there.

MRS DARLING: I need you to hold me.

(She runs to wrap her arms around him. He shakes her off.)

MRS DARLING: Please!

GEORGE: Goodbye, honey. You're still the love of my life.

(They struggle, GEORGE pushes her away and heads out the door. Exits)

MRS DARLING: *(Calling out door)* George?

GEORGE: Nana? Nana, are you gone too? Anyone!

MOTHER: *(Entering in shimmering light)* Don't worry, sweetie, Mama's here.

MRS DARLING: You? No!

MOTHER: They're all gone now, little one. They've left you all alone, my poor poor baby, but Mama's here to take away the pain. Come to Mama, I'll make it all better.

MRS DARLING: Better? No, wait ! I'm not going to trust you again...I don't really see you. This is a delusion. The voice of my despair. Just a voice in my head. That's all.

MOTHER: Shh, shh. Don't be afraid to believe. Without magic, there'd only be lasagna and dust busters!

MRS DARLING: Go! Even if you're not here, I don't want you!

MOTHER: Sure you do. George off for the mountains and your children like fireflies, blinking, blinking...

MRS DARLING: You're voice rattles in my head like snake scales.

MOTHER: I've just got a touch of laryngitis. Do you mind if I sit down, sweetie? I was bowling in the house of fear and pain and when I heard you call!

MRS DARLING: NOT FOR YOU!

MOTHER: Better not hurt mother's feelings.

MRS DARLING: You're dead! I buried you in Newark!

MOTHER: And you expected me to stay? Oh come on. Don't be a naughty girl. Let Mother kiss away the tears and put a band aid on the boobos. We'll have ice cream. Do you still like pistachio?

MRS DARLING: No!

MOTHER: Don't shrink away from Mother, you stinky little petunia. Come on. Put your head on Mama's lap, and Mother will stroke your pretty hair.

MRS DARLING: I...I want to...but I'm afraid to touch you.

MOTHER: Oh honey, afraid of Mama? Think if you touch me you'll burst into flames and burn 'til your skin crackles? Well, maybe. But then again, we can still have fun. I brought you a special visitor. One from far away.

MRS DARLING: You did? You really did? IS IT WENDY!

MOTHER: Don't be ridiculous. I brought Dolly! *(Produces doll)*

MRS DARLING: Oh. My dolly! But if you found Dolly, you can find anyone!

MOTHER: Maybe, baby. Let's have a little sing to cheer you up, and then we'll talk. *(Singing to doll)*
Skida ma rink a dink a dink skidamarinka a doo
I love you
Skidamarinka dink a dink skidamarinka doo...
Come on honey!

MRS DARLING: *(Joins in)* I love you
I love you in the morning and in the afternoon
I love you in the evening and underneath the moon...

MOTHER: *(Sings and MRS DARLING tries to follow)*
I love you when I'm bowling,
I love you when I'm dead.
I love you when I'm killing you
And chopping off your head!

MRS DARLING: Chopping off my head?

MOTHER: No no no, honey, Dolly's head.

MRS DARLING: It didn't sound that way.

MOTHER: That's because you never listen! It's so hard for you to listen because you are just a little bit selfish. Everything is all about you you you, you little drama queen. I mean, what do you want? Mama's placenta so you can squeeze out the cord blood?

MRS DARLING: Mother, whatever you're here for I'll give it to you.

MOTHER: Really?

MRS DARLING: Anything!

MOTHER: Alright. Well, let's if you really mean it. So...how 'bout you sacrifice a petite piggy.

MRS DARLING: A piggy?

MOTHER: A sweet, little, milky, white pig who's never got her hands dirty, who calls for the car, and calls for her supper, and calls for her fiddlers three.

MRS DARLING: Me?

MOTHER: Ever clever!

MRS DARLING: Sacrifice me?

MOTHER: You got that gun?

MRS DARLING: What?

MOTHER: G as in genocide, U as in undertaker and N as in nasturtium!

MRS DARLING: A gun? You're going to kill me... with a gun?

MOTHER: Oh you're always jumping to conclusions. You're going to kill yourself! Be proactive!

MRS DARLING: That's what I have to do?

MOTHER: Sure. Don't you see sweetie? It's the only way. Do you remember Penelope? Your little apricot poodle,

with the stumpy tail, who never stopped yapping?
Well, she didn't move to the country.

MRS DARLING: You fiend!

MOTHER: And neither did your kids.

MRS DARLING: WHAT DOES THAT MEAN?

MOTHER: Mother can't stand to see your pain. Kill
yourself, sweetie. You'll feel so much better.

MRS DARLING: You want me dead?

MOTHER: Sure.

MRS DARLING: No way.

MOTHER: Nothing changes. Egotistical, vain. Rotten to
the core. But Mother doesn't judge. Mother forgives all.
Only mother loves you, no matter what. So, have you
even asked how Mother's feeling?

MRS DARLING: No.

MOTHER: Not well. Not well at all. Mama's very lonely,
no one to zip my zippers. And I miss you, baby. Come
to Mama, I need a side kick, a grave slave a shade with
a ready ear. Be my sweet girly, my own gravey slavey.
Come on, come on get that gun.

MRS DARLING: What gun?

MOTHER: Naughty girl. You can't trick Mother!
(Pulls gun from drawer) I know, I know you've lost
so much, bunny, But here it is! *(Mouth noises)* Click,
click, mother's comfort

(Brandishing gun and handing it to MRS DARLING*)*

MOTHER: Loaded for convenience and easy handling.
Take it. A tiny squeeze, and boom! Make the whole
world go away! You've done your best, baby, you don't
deserve to suffer. Come to Mamma, you nasty girl, and
we'll have a little fun.

MRS DARLING: So lonely, it's almost worse than dying.

MOTHER: I know, baby. I've got an extra clip in my bag just in case.

MRS DARLING: Mother?

MOTHER: Come on. Feel it in your hand, The pure relief of cold steel It's a sweet little piece. There's nothing too good for my baby.

MRS DARLING: Mother? Is it going to hurt?

MOTHER: Hurt? Oh it's lovely. Like the sun. It hardly hurts at all, it's just exquisite, why, in barely a moment, bang! Flash! You're light as air. Hurt? Oh it's lovely. Like...the sun

(MRS DARLING *holds up gun.*)

MOTHER: That's it! Come on, come on, this doesn't require a lot of thought! Do it, you wretched girl!

MRS DARLING: I have to be sure.

MOTHER: Nothing is a sure bet. Just give it your best shot. Come on, you little trollop. I don't believe you love me at all. You're dawdling around while I suffer! You know how I hate to wait.

MRS DARLING: Am I going to eternity with you?

MOTHER: Maybe, baby, let's get you to the other side! Get on with it, little fraidy cat.

(*From offstage, girl's laughter*)

MRS DARLING: Did you hear that?

MOTHER: I didn't hear anything. Come on, you stink of tears and your mascara's run.

MRS DARLING: (*Runs to mirror*) I look...who cares how I look?

MOTHER: You don't care? Then you're dead already!

(Laughter)

MRS DARLING: Get out of my way! *(Calling)* Wendy? Is that you? Are you angry at Mommy? I am so sorry. Please, come home. I'll give you a perfect party, Wendy? Do you want hats and streamers or are you too old for all that? *(Starts running around)*

MOTHER: Think you'll find them? They're lost in the latitudes. There is no neverland and there is no pole except in Poland.

MRS DARLING: In Poland?

MOTHER: Oh honey, you are desperate.

(MRS DARLING begins to run around arranging imaginary table)

MRS DARLING: Wendy? Come on, sweetie, you can't miss your own party. Wendy? My hummingbird? I'm going to make it all up to you, honey.

(Music)

MRS DARLING: Oh! Thank you. *(Dances)*

MOTHER: Hola! Let's dance 'til dawn!

(MRS DARLING dances, MOTHER dances next to her, mimicking. A girl's laughter. MRS DARLING freezes.)

MRS DARLING: Oh Wendy! *(Springs back to dancing)* Here, look! I'll teach you. Like this.

MOTHER: Is that the cha- cha?

MRS DARLING: *(She dances franticly then collapses. Music stops.)* WENDY! Please!

MOTHER: A party, dancing, it's all very nice. But it's the bullet you need to bring them all back. It's the ping and the snap as your synapses go black. Don't you see, baby? Time's a wasting, little fool, and you're wasting

my time. *(Waves gun around)* Take it. No? Here,
I'll leave it and you can use it later.

MRS DARLING: No!

MOTHER: No? Well suit yourself, you always do.
But mother's got to go. Oh, don't look so sad sweetie,
your bed of thorns is ready and Mama will wait.
(She fades away)

MRS DARLING: Mother? Mother?

(Girls laughter)

MRS DARLING: Wendy! *(Gets up. Shouting into intercom)*
Wendy! Hello! Hello! Hello! Are you there? Oh very
funny. Torture Mommy.

(Barking)

MRS DARLING: That dog again. She misses Daddy!
STOP THE NOISE!

(GEORGE reenters with Nana.)

GEORGE: I can't leave you. So I called and made a deal.
I gave up Harry.

MRS DARLING: *(To mirror)* The mirror is empty. My eyes
are gone, there's only the whiteness of bone. I am the
dragon who has eaten her own tail and disappeared.
Everyone is gone!

GEORGE: Not me. *(Holds out arms)* Come here.

(She shrinks away.)

MRS DARLING: I'm untouchable.

GEORGE: I wouldn't say that.

(Takes her in his arms)

MRS DARLING: Oh!

GEORGE: Yes.

MRS DARLING: You're really here?

GEORGE: Yes.

MRS DARLING: And the kids?

GEORGE: They're really gone.

(Knocking, MRS DARLING *and* GEORGE *freeze in embrace.)*

(Enter JETHRO *and* PROSPERA.*)*

PROSPERA: The door was open....

JETHRO: Have no fear. We're here to help you.

GEORGE: Who are you?

JETHRO: Representatives of a new order. I am Jethro and this is my companion Prospera.

MRS DARLING: Messengers! From my children!

GEORGE: They don't look like messengers.

PROSPERA: Oh honey. Don't expect little visitors.

MRS DARLING: That sounds so...final!

JETHRO: Quick. Give her an affirmation.

PROSPERA: You are a beautiful, loving, creative person.

MRS DARLING: How do you know?

PROSPERA: You deserve the best, and the best is coming to you now.

GEORGE: I told you, Honey.

MRS DARLING: My children?

JETHRO: Gone.

MRS DARLING: *(Shocked)* Forever?

JETHRO: That's why we are here. To liberate you from shame. To affirm your goodness and to embrace you.

PROSPERA: Come. Give us your hands. Let us heal you.

JETHRO: We need you.

GEORGE & MRS DARLING: Need us?

JETHRO: We need you to forgive yourself.

PROSPERA: And we need your good looks, money, and social connections. We know all about your work with the orphans. So effective! We admire your tenacity and your fund raising ability, and we want you to be our spokespersons. Nationally and internationally.

JETHRO: Parents of the lost children, what a handsome pair.

MRS DARLING: They're not lost, they left us!

JETHRO: Well, we cannot control the behavior of others.

GEORGE: Who exactly are you?

PROSPERA: We are the founders of Parents Without Children.

PROSPERA & JETHRO: If they have left us, we forgive them. If we have left them, we forgive ourselves.

JETHRO: Celebrate life!

PROSPERA: Yes! Affirmations! Affirmations! I am whole and complete within myself. I love and appreciate myself just the way I am. Every day I'm getting better and better. My life is blossoming into total perfection. Children are obstacles cast before us on the path to self-realization. Love yourself.

MRS DARLING: No!

GEORGE: Don't be so negative. Try it.

MRS DARLING: If...I say those things. About my infinite creative power...will it bring my babies back?

JETHRO: Transcend them. Find the inner peace that you deserve.

PROSPERA: Forgiveness is the only way to heal.

MRS DARLING: How can I forgive myself? I've driven away my children!

JETHRO: Let go of loss and see it for what it is. Enlightenment. We are all energy.
  We are all one.

MRS DARLING: You mean one with our children? Our children are always with us?

PROSPERA: That's it! You don't need the children themselves! You need them as companions for your inner child, they can all be in there together. Why, right now they might all be playing Go Fish!

JETHRO: You are the treasure on your map.

PROSPERA: Our spokeswoman. Mother of the lost children. Queen of her own enlightenment.

MRS DARLING: Do you really think so?

PROSPERA: Articulate, perfect bones, a great wardrobe, fantastic connections.

GEORGE: What about me?

JETHRO: Father of the lost children. Nobility, grace and membership in all the right clubs. You can soar once you dedicate yourself to a higher purpose.

GEORGE: All I have to do is find it.

JETHRO: You will find it. Use your inner compass. Come. Repeat after me...

(All four hold hands. GEORGE *and* MRS DARLING *close eyes and repeat after* JETHRO *and* PROSPERA.)*

PROSPERA & JETHRO: I am now releasing my past.

GEORGE & MRS DARLING: I am now releasing my past.

PROSPERA & JETHRO: I am now dissolving all negative, limiting beliefs. I now forgive and release everyone in my life.

GEORGE & MRS DARLING: I am now dissolving all
negative...

PROSPERA & JETHRO: All negative, limiting beliefs.
I now forgive and release everyone in my life.

GEORGE: I now forgive and release everyone in my life.
You, Harry, for screwing me. Hey, I screwed you back.
And...my lawyer for selling me out. And all the little
people who conspired to bring me down...

JETHRO: Thank you George. And you, little flower?

MRS DARLING: I now forgive and release everyone
in my life. Including you, Mother, and you, George,
that's right. And...and you, children, for leaving me.
Oh! I feel so good!

PROSPERA: You see?

MRS DARLING: What now?

JETHRO: There's cameras outside.

MRS DARLING: Got that blue shirt, honey?

GEORGE: Why not?

*(Whips it out of his briefcase. Puts it on. MRS DARLING
looks on with approval.)*

PROSPERA: You, you look marvelous already.
But perhaps a touchup...

MRS DARLING: Oh! But my hair! *(Runs to mirror.
Looks in mirror. Smiles. Puts on lipstick sloppily)*

JETHRO: Wonderful!

MRS DARLING: *(Putting on coat over nightgown)* Parents
Without Children. Perhaps "sans" would give it that
special appeal. P S C. Parents "sans" Children.

MRS DARLING: *(Back to mirror)* With all this suffering,
I'm sure I've lost weight.

PROSPERA: You look beautiful. Gaunt. Suffering is so good for the complexion.

GEORGE: P S C Spokesperson? Can I be chair of the board?

JETHRO: Of course.

GEORGE: Thank you.

MRS DARLING: *(Putting on shoes)* So here are my shoes...real alligator. My mother taught me, you can never invest badly in accessories!

PROSPERA: Perfect!

(Cries a little, wipes away tears, smiles. Links arms with GEORGE)

GEORGE: We're now creating our lives exactly the way we want them, and we don't have to please anyone else because, hey, we're willing to be happy. We really do deserve the best in life! We deserve to have it all. And I know because my inner wisdom is guiding me. And what we've lost, hey, we didn't really lose anything! Whatever life takes away from you, let it go.

MRS DARLING: So children...thank you for being and thank you for going. There, we're ready!

(To black)

END OF PLAY

www.ingramcontent.com/pod-product-compliance
Lightning Source LLC
Chambersburg PA
CBHW070027110426
42741CB00034B/2667